Austrian Macroeconomics:
A Diagrammatical Exposition

Roger W. Garrison
Graphics by Cheryl L. Mallory

The Ludwig von Mises Institute
Auburn, Alabama
2010

This essay is published for the first time here and, concurrently, as a chapter in *New Directions in Austrian Economics* (Kansas City: Sheed Andrews and McMeel, 1978), a volume in the Studies in Economic Theory series. The essay was included in a symposium on Austrian economics held at Windsor Castle in September 1976, which was cosponsored by the University College at Buckingham and the Institute for Humane Studies.

ISBN: 978-1-61016-007-0

Austrian Macroeconomics: A Diagrammatical Exposition

INTRODUCTION

The object of this paper is the development of a diagrammatic model representing the Austrian view of macroeconomic relationships. More explicitly, the model will be designed to faithfully reflect the macroeconomic relationships found in the writings of Mises,[1] Hayek,[2] and Rothbard.[3] At this stage in its development the model is little more than a skeletal outline. It is a framework that can facilitate a fuller discussion of the actual adjustment mechanisms—the processes by which the economy is moved toward an equilibrium position. Because of the brevity of such discussions in this paper, the model may appear to be unfaithful to the Austrian view in one respect: It focuses on aggregates rather than on processes. Hopefully, this unfaithfulness is only apparent. Although the model is constructed with aggregate quantities and deals with the relationships between these quantities, no attempt is made to "explain" one aggregate in terms of another. It is fully recognized that, ultimately, each aggregate must be explained or accounted for in terms of the individual choices and actions of market participants. It is in this sense that the model is consistent with the methodological individualism so characteristic of Austrian theory.

Before we begin the actual construction of the model, a preview of some of its primary characteristics may be in order. The purpose of the preview is twofold. Firstly, it will suggest that the model is in fact worth developing. Many of the following characteristics are desirable ones and give the Austrian model an edge over the more orthodox models. Secondly, it should help those readers uninitiated in Austrian macroeconomics to follow the development of the model more easily.

1. The capital stock in Austrian theory is made up of heterogeneous capital. The relationship between the various pieces of capital can be one of substitutability or complementarity. The individual pieces of capital (both fixed and circulating) are integrated into a "structure of production." (Although the nature of capital is obscured by simplifying assumptions in the first section of this paper, it is taken into account more fully in subsequent sections.)

2. The size of the capital stock is treated as a variable in the model. The usual assumption is that even though investment of some positive amount is realized each period, the stock of capital remains constant.[4] With the Austrian model this assumption is unnecessary. This has the important consequence of integrating macroeconomic theory, growth theory, and business cycle theory. Explanations of both growth and cyclical activity are based on the same macroeconomic model.

3. The Austrian model is not a full-employment model in the sense that it assumes full employment. The analysis does begin however, with an economy that is fully employed: "[W]e have to start where general economic theory stops; that is to say at a condition of equilibrium when no unused resources exist. The existence of unused resources is itself a fact which needs explanation."[5] The model does in fact explain the abnormally high

levels of unemployment that accompany the contraction phase of the business cycle.

4. The Austrian model takes explicit account of the time element in the production process. It does not simply add "lags" as an afterthought to an otherwise timeless model. It accounts for the fact that production takes time and that more production takes more time.

5. Austrian macroeconomic theory is not a theory of real income determination. Ultimately, it is a theory of co-ordination[6]—of how the production process is co-ordinated with the tastes of individuals (their time and liquidity preferences), and how monetary disturbances affect this co-ordination. Because of its focus on the co-ordination problem, there is no *sharp* distinction between Austrian macroeconomics and Austrian microeconomics.

THE STRUCTURE OF PRODUCTION

One of the most distinctive features of Austrian macroeconomic theory is its use of the concept of a "structure of production."[7] This concept was formulated to give explicit recognition to the notion that capital (and the capital structure) has two dimensions. It has a value dimension which can be expressed in monetary terms, and it has a time dimension which is an expression of the time that elapses between the application of the "original means of production"[8] (labor and land) and the eventual emergence of the consumption goods associated with them. The development of the notion of two-dimensional capital has its roots, of course, in the writings of Jevons.[9] It can be traced from Jevons to Cassel[10] and Böhm-Bawerk[11] and then to Mises,[12] and from Mises to Hayek,[13] Rothbard,[14] and other contemporary Austrian theorists. This view of capital, then, is neither new nor is it strictly Austrian, yet the notion of two-dimensional capital is by no means readily accepted by capital theorists in general.

A third though not independent dimension of capital can be envisaged which represents a composite of the two dimensions described above. Again, Jevons was the first to synthesize this third dimension. He made the distinction between the "quantity of capital" and the "length of time during which it remains invested." He then devised the third dimension of capital by " .. multiplying each portion of capital invested at any moment by the length of time for which it remains invested."[15] The compounding of interest was ignored for the sake of simplicity. The resulting composite dimension was shown to have the units of "dollar-years." (The units are Americanized here. Jevons, of course, used "pound-years.")[16]

Cassel followed thirty years later with a similar formulation: " . . . interest is paid in proportion to the capital lent and in proportion to the duration of the loan, i.e., in proportion to the *product* of value and time" (emphasis added).[17] Cassel's product and Jevons's composite dimension measure the same thing. They are indications of the extent to which capital is "tied-up" in the production process. No claim is made here that this product can be calculated directly, but if we can conceive of interest income and of the rate of interest, then we can conceive of this composite dimension of capital—the amount of "waiting" or postponement of consumption brought about by the payment of interest.

This composite dimension will be referred to as "aggregate production time"[18] or simply as "production time." For sure there are problems in aggregating (even conceptually) the production time associated with different pieces of capital just as there are problems with all macroeconomic aggregates. Much ambiguity will be avoided, however, by using the concept of *aggregate* production time rather than *average* production time or *average* period of production. These latter concepts were used by both Jevons[19] and Böhm-Bawerk,[20] but were rejected by Mises,[21] Hayek,[22] and Rothbard.[23] Many of the problems of Böhm-Bawerk's capital theory had their roots in his use of the

6

average period of production: Because the denominator of his average was the value dimension of the structure of production (value reckoned in labor units), and because changes in the numerator of his average are typically accompanied by changes in the denominator in the same direction, the direction of change in the average period of production is generally ambiguous. Further problems derive from Böhm-Bawerk's incautious generalizations about changes in the average period of production that were based on the analysis of an oversimplified model.

With a full awareness of the difficulties of working with aggregates in general and of working with aggregate production time in particular, the structure of production will be defined in terms of the value of the capital at each stage in the production process and the aggregate production time associated with the process. The difficulties encountered by Böhm-Bawerk will be avoided by relying on a somewhat less rigorous interpretation of "changes in aggregate production time," but discussion of this interpretation will be deferred to a later section of the paper. The actual modeling can begin with an examination of earlier treatments of the structure of production.

The first graphical representation of the structure of production in the Austrian literature is found in *Prices and Production* in the form of the famous Hayekian triangles.[24] Such a triangle has been reproduced in Figure 1. (The axes have been reversed for convenience of exposition.) Hayek envisaged a vertically integrated production process in which the " . . . original means of production are expended continuously during the whole process of production."[25] Again, "original means" refers to the non-produced (or non-reproducible) means of production, i.e., to labor and land. (In our discussion we will associate the original means with "laborers" and the produced means with "capitalists." The terms laborers and capitalists, of course, are used in a functional sense and do not refer to particular individuals.) The production process begins at point T in Figure 1 and proceeds leftward. At the conclusion of the process consumption goods with a dollar value of OY emerge. At point T no capital exists. At point D, one of the intermediate stages of production, there exists capital with a dollar value of *DD'*. This capital can be viewed as simply the unfinished consumption goods that will be valued at *OY* when the production process is completed.

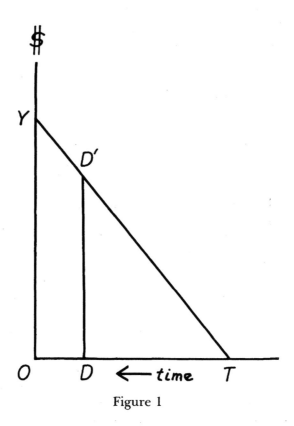

Figure 1

The Hayekian triangle has two mutually re-enforcing interpretations.[26] On the one hand, it can depict the flow of capital in real time from its inception at point *T* through the numerous stages of production until it emerges as consumption goods valued at *OY*. This is the interpretation adopted in the preceding paragraph. On the other hand, if the production process is in equilibrium, or to be more vivid, if it is in the state referred to by

Mises as the "evenly rotating economy,"[27] then the triangle represents all of the various stages of production that co-exist at each and every point in time. At any given point in time, for instance, consumption goods OY will be emerging from the production process, and at the same time the unfinished goods DD' will be in existence destined to emerge at a later date as consumption goods.

The dollar amount represented by DD' is less than that represented by OY for two reasons. Firstly, additional quantities of the original means (i.e., labor) are yet to be applied to the unfinished product that exists at point D. Secondly, OY and DD' represent consumption goods available at different points in time. If OY is available now, DD' will be available for consumption only at some future date. DD', then, is discounted with respect to OY. To separate these two influences on the value of DD' with respect to OY, the model will be modified. Instead of conceiving, as Hayek did, of a process in which the original means of production are applied continuously, we will conceive of a production process in which the original means are applied only at the beginning of the process. The Hayekian triangle is abandoned in favor of a trapezoid. In Figure 2, the production process begins at point T with the application of labor services having a dollar value of TF. These original means grow in value as they pass through the numerous stages of production, finally emerging as consumption goods valued at OY dollars.

A second modification has been made in Figure 2. The horizontal axis now represents the aggregate production time (APT) associated with the structure of production. This allows the relaxation of the assumption that the structure is characterized by complete vertical integration. The slope of line FY, then, represents the rate of increase in value per unit of time per dollar invested at point T. That is, the slope of line FY is the (simple) rate of interest (profit) when the economy is in equilibrium.

Of course, this is a highly stylized representation of the actual structure of production. The development of the Austrian model, however, will be accompanied by discussions of the actual processes that take place in the real-world structure of produc-

9

tion. These discussions will recognize that capital and labor services are applied in each of the stages of production. Changes in the structure, for instance, will be couched in terms of labor

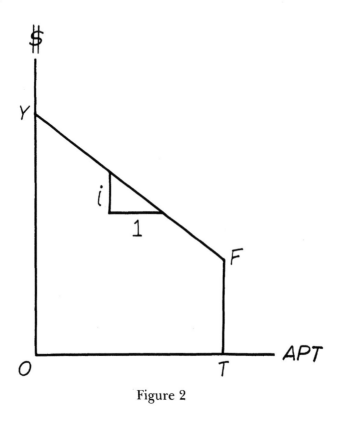

Figure 2

and capital being moved out of the stages relatively close to the final (consumption) stage and into stages relatively remote from the consumption stage (or *vice versa*) in response to (intertemporal) price changes and profit opportunities. This corresponds to a lengthening (or shortening) of the structure. Changes in the shape of the stylized representation of the structure of production will be an indication of the nature of the changes in the real-world structure.

INTERTEMPORAL EXCHANGE

Intertemporal exchange is the exchange of present consumption goods for future consumption goods and *vice versa*. This type of market transaction is generally introduced by first allowing for pure consumption loans only. Investment loans are brought into view only after consumption loans have established some initial terms of trade in the intertemporal market. The Austrian model, though, will account for intertemporal exchange by initially abstracting from the pure consumption loan. This will allow us to focus on the type of intertemporal exchange that is inherent in the production process. The intertemporal market, then, can be thought of as dealing with direct purchases of investment goods as well as with loans made for the purpose of purchasing investment goods.

In the context of the present model intertemporal exchange can be accounted for in terms of the original means of production, i.e., in terms of the market for labor services. The labor services represent future consumption goods, which is to say that they can be converted into consumption goods only by allowing them to pass through the time-consuming production process. Laborers sell their services (future consumption goods) receiving in exchange dollars that can be used to purchase presently existing consumption goods. The sale of labor services, then, constitutes the demand for present goods (and the supply of future goods). Looking at the other side of the market for intertemporal exchange, the labor services are purchased by the capitalists. The capitalists exchange dollars for labor services and, *ipso facto*, register a demand for future goods. At the same time they constitute the supply of present goods. (Of course, this is an "excess" supply: At the end of the production process the capitalists own OY of consumption goods. They consume $OY-TF$ and supply the remaining TF to the laborers.)

The supply and demand for present goods are represented diagrammatically in Figure 3. This market for intertemporal exchange is equilibrated by adjustments in the intertemporal price ratio—the rate of interest. The particular shape and posi-

11

tioning of these curves is determined by the individuals' (laborers' and capitalists') relative evaluations of present as opposed to future goods, i.e., by their time preferences. The *technical* aspects of transforming the labor services into consumption goods, as might be represented by a technical transformation function, are kept in the background here. The Austrian model focuses not on the technical considerations *per se* but rather on the alternative combinations of present and future goods that indi-

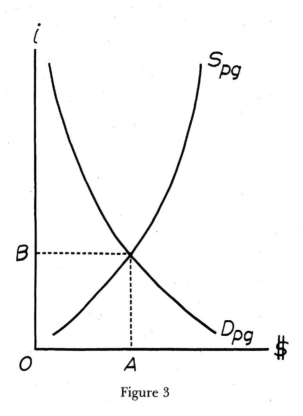

Figure 3

viduals perceive to be possible. Of course, when the economy is in equilibrium (the Misesian evenly rotating economy), individuals *know* what alternatives are possible so that the transformations that are perceived to be possible and the actual transactions formations are one and the same. When the economy is out of equilibrium, however, individuals will act on the basis of what they perceive the possibilities to be and not on the basis of what the possibilities actually are in some technological sense. This (fundamentally Austrian) distinction is an important one and will come into play in understanding the workings of the Austrian model under disequilibrium conditions.

Rothbard makes use of a diagram essentially identical to the one in Figure 3.[28] He points out that the intersection of the two curves determines the equilibrium rate of interest and the equilibrium amount of (gross) savings. (Net savings are zero.) Given the stylized structure of production of the present model, these (gross) savings manifest themselves as payments for labor services. When the economy is in equilibrium, the rate of interest is given by OB; the total payment for labor services by OA.

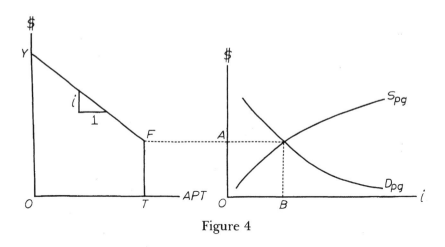

Figure 4

It should be noted at this point that OA in Figure 3 measures the same payment that is measured by TF in Figure 2. In recognition of this connection between the market for intertemporal exchange and the structure of production, Figure 3 can be inverted, rotated, and juxtaposed with Figure 2 to yield the summary diagram shown in Figure 4. There is a second connec-

13

tion between the two panels of Figure 4. The rate of interest is represented by *OB* in the right-hand panel and by the slope of the line *FY* in the left-hand panel. In equilibrium, of course, these two representations must reflect the same rate of interest.

It may be helpful at this point to show the relationship between this simple Austrian model and the corresponding Keynesian model. The point of commonality is the magnitude *OY* which represents the equilibrium dollar value of consumption goods. In the simple Keynesian model point *Y* is the intersection of the consumption function and the 45° reference line. *OY* is the distance from that intersection to the horizontal (or vertical) axis. Figure 5 shows the two models drawn on vertical planes perpendicular to one another and intersecting along *OY*. (This comparison may do some violence to the Keynesian model in that all magnitudes are expressed in dollar terms rather than real terms.)

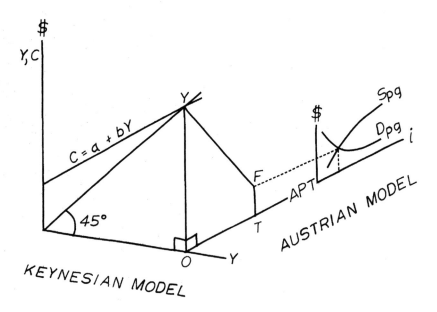

Figure 5

INVESTMENT

In order to deal with (net) investment an additional relationship must be introduced into the model, namely the relationship between the quantity of capital (dollar value) in the structure of production and the production time associated with it. ("Quantity of capital" here refers to *all* the capital in the structure of production. In Figure 2 it referred to the quantity that exists *at each stage* of the structure of production.) Although these two dimensions of the structure of production (quantity of capital and production time) are defined independently of one another, there is, according to Austrian theory, a relationship between them. Again, this relationship has its genesis in the writings of Jevons: "Capital simply allows us to expend labor in advance."[29] *More* capital, Jevons went on to show, allows us to expend labor *further* in advance.[30]

The positive relationship between capital and production time has suffered several set-backs during its development. Böhm-Bawerk, for instance, couched it in terms of the "average period of production," inadvertently causing the formulation to be ambiguous. But Mises and the contemporary Austrian theorists (e.g., Hayek and Rothbard) fully recognize the errors in Böhm-Bawerk's formulation.[31] They still accept, however, the basic notion that there is a positive relationship between the quantity of capital and the production time associated with it. Mises, for instance, argues that " . . . every increase in the supply of capital goods available results in a lengthening of the period of production, and of waiting time, . . ."[32] and conversely that " . . . [a]n increase in the quantity of capital goods available is a necessary condition for the adoption of processes in which the period of production and therefore waiting time are longer."[33] Similar statements can be found in Rothbard's formulation: "Any increase in capital goods can serve only to lengthen the structure, i.e., to enable the adoption of longer . . . processes."[34]

Hayek points out the difficulties of talking about "changes in the period of production" when the term refers to the actual aggregation of investment periods. He goes on, though, to say that

> ... since the use of the expression "changes in the length of the process" is a convenient way of describing the type of changes in the whole process where the changes in the investment periods are predominantly in one direction, there is probably something to be said for retaining it, provided that it is used cautiously. . . .[35]

With this somewhat less rigorous view "changes in production time" is more of a "shorthand" for the type of changes being made to the structure of production than a change in a genuine aggregate.

The relationship between the quantity of capital and production time has been called into question in recent years by the so-called "double-switching and capital-reversing debates."[36] The possibility of capital reversing (which involves an apparent violation of the Austrian relationship) has been the source of much controversy in Cambridge capital theory. Although there is good reason to believe that the problems created by double switching and capital reversing are confined to the Cambridge paradigm itself, the Austrian model will eventually have to be defended against the Cambridge charges. But this task will not be undertaken here. Rather, our concern with the problem will end with the observation that even those who think that capital reversing is possible consider it extremely unlikely: "[Capital reversing] could happen, but it looks like being on the edge of things that could happen."[37] (!)

The positive relationship between the quantity of capital (dollar value) and production time is introduced diagrammatically in the upper panel of Figure 6. The "wavy" shape of the curve is simply a way of indicating that no claims are made about the rate of change in the slope of the curve. The only significant feature of the curve is that its slope is positive. That the curve should begin at the origin seems obvious enough: There can be no production time if there is no capital. The origin, then, may represent the hand-to-mouth existence of a Robinson Crusoe,

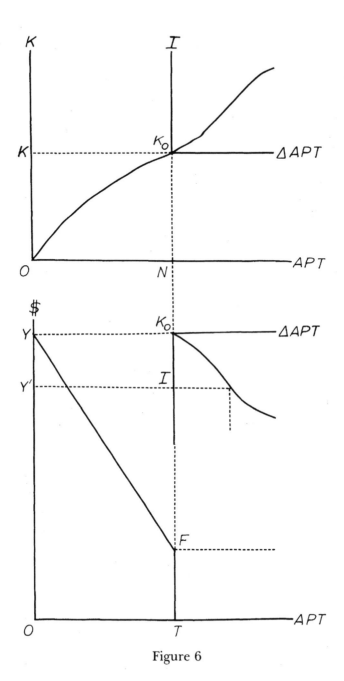

Figure 6

but for purposes of developing the Austrian model, this is a trivial aspect of the diagram.

The "initial" production time is OT as indicated in the lower panel of Figure 6. This panel, of course, is the now-familiar structure of production. (The word "initial" is used here in an arbitrary sense: It does not refer to the starting point of the production process but rather to the starting point of our analysis.) The initial dollar value of capital corresponding to production time OT is represented by OK in the upper panel.

If the origin in the upper panel is shifted from O to K_0, then the portion of the curve extending northeastward from K_0 will represent the relationship between *investment* and *changes* in production time. This is the relevant portion of the curve. The term "investment" in the Austrian model is defined in a slightly unorthodox manner. It is not the *rate* of increase in the quantity of capital, but rather the addition of a quantity of capital measured with respect to the initial quantity K_0. It is measured in dollars rather than dollars per year.

At this stage in the construction of the model, investment can come about only at the expense of consumption. (Investment made possible by the creation of new credit will be dealt with in the following section.) The relationship between investment and consumption can be shown by inverting the northeast portion of the upper panel and lowering it until the horizontal axis is aligned with point Y of the structure of production. If an investment of K_0I is made, for instance, it is made at the expense of consumption YY'. In view of the fact that investment is to be an endogenous variable in the Austrian model, it is probably preferable to state the relationship in another way. If a change in an exogenous variable brings about an investment of K_0I, it, *ipso facto*, brings about a decrease in consumption of YY'.

The diagrammatics developed to this point are shown in Figure 7. This model allows us to determine the changes in the structure of production that are brought about by shifts in the supply and demand curves of the intertemporal market. These shifts can be thought of as resulting from changes in individuals' relative evaluation of present as opposed to future goods, i.e.,

18

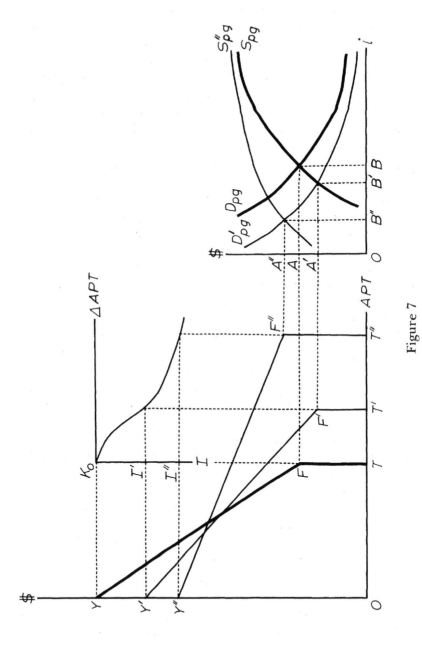

Figure 7

19

changes in their time preferences. A decrease in the time preferences of laborers, for example, can be represented by a shift in the demand for present goods from D_{pg} to D'_{pg}, which intersects the original supply-of-present-goods curve at coordinates OA' and OB'. (To this point the magnitude OA has been taken to represent both the amount paid for labor services and the dollar value of present goods consumed by laborers. For this equality to hold requires the tacit assumption that laborers are neither increasing nor decreasing their cash holdings. However, if the demand for present goods shifts without causing a corresponding shift in the supply of present goods (demand for future goods), then there must be a change in the cash holdings of laborers (from Walras's Law). That is, a shift in just one of the two curves, D_{pg} and S_{pg}, must correspond to a change in both time and liquidity preferences. OA, then, represents the dollar value of present goods consumed by laborers—which equals the amount paid to laborers minus the change in their cash holdings. (For our immediate purposes, though, this change in cash holdings will be kept in the background.)

The diagrammatic representation of the structure of production is uniquely determined by the shift in the demand for present goods. The amount of present goods advanced to laborers is now $T'F'$ ($=OA'$), and the new equilibrium rate of interest is OB' ($<OB$), which is reflected as a less steep slope in the structure of production diagram. (The slope of $F'Y'$ is less than the slope of FY.) An investment of K_oI' is realized, which involves an increase in production time of TT'. In other words, the decrease in the time preferences (of laborers) has allowed resources that would otherwise have been used for current consumption to be used instead for investment purposes. The accompanying decrease in the rate of interest has made it profitable to employ these resources in more time-consuming methods of production.

In the real-world structure of production the actual process might be described as follows: Capitalists in their entrepreneurial roles sense that individuals are now willing to forgo consumption in the near future in order to achieve even greater consumption in the more distant future. This change in time preferences

20

creates profit opportunities that cause the capitalists to bid capital and labor services away from the stages of production relatively close to the final (consumption) stage and into stages relatively remote from the consumption stage. They are also induced by the lowering of the interest rate to create additional stages that had previously been unprofitable.[38]

Although the dollar expenditure on consumption goods decreases from OY to OY', consumption in real terms decreases only temporarily and then rises to a new high once the additional investment comes to fruition. It is this additional quantity of consumption goods coming into the market, of course, that allows the prices of consumption goods to be bid down to a level consistent with OY'.

The above description of changes in the structure of production brought about by a decrease in time preferences is very similar to the discussion found in *Prices and Production* of the change in the shape of a Hayekian triangle brought about by voluntary savings:

If we compare the two diagrams [representing the structure of production before and after the change in voluntary savings] we see at once that the nature of the change consists in a stretching [of the structure]. . . . Its [height at the final stage], which measures the amount of money spent during the period of time on consumers' goods, . . . has permanently decreased. . . . This means that the price of a unit of consumers' goods, the output of which has increased as a consequence of the more capitalistic methods of production, will fall. . . . The amount of money spent in each of the later stages of production has also decreased, while the amount used in the earlier stages has increased, and the total spent on intermediate products has increased also because of the addition of . . . new stage[s] of production.[39]

Although the price level and the real level of consumption are accounted for in the discussion of the workings of the Austrian model, they do not appear in the diagrammatical representation in any explicit form. Austrian macroeconomics has never been concerned directly with the general price *level*, but has been concerned instead with the *relative* price of consumption goods as opposed to investment goods—or, in terms of the present model, the *relative* amounts paid for consumption goods as opposed to labor services. This is a fundamental aspect of Austrian theory that sets it apart from the more orthodox macroeconomic theory. Patinkin, for instance, lumps "consumer commodities" and "investment commodities" into a single aggregate and then tells us that " . . . [t]he prices of these two categories are assumed to change in the same proportion."[40] By disallowing relative price changes between these two categories of commodities, Patinkin puts the structure of production in a straightjacket. This throws the entire burden of moving the economy from one equilibrium position to another on the real cash balance effect.[41]

A shift in the supply of present goods from S_{pg} to $S_{pg}{}''$ could be the result of a decrease in the time preferences of capitalists. The effects of this shift on the structure of production can be analyzed in the same manner and with similar results. The new equilibrium (associated with $D_{pg}{}'$ and $S_{pg}{}''$) is shown with double-prime notation. The only significant difference is that the amount of present goods consumed by laborers has increased when before it decreased. But this difference was to be expected: A decrease in the time preferences of *laborers* means that they are willing to consume *fewer* present goods now in order to enjoy greater (real) consumption later; a decrease in the time preferences of *capitalists* means that they are willing to advance *more* present goods to laborers now in order to enjoy more (real) consumption later.

A change in time preferences is not the only change in tastes that can cause a shift in the supply and demand for present goods, although it seems to be the one that the Austrian theorists are most concerned with. But shifts of the curves can also result from changes in the demand for money, e.g., from increases or decreases in liquidity preferences. (Hayek was aware in his early writings of the need to incorporate the analysis of liquidity preferences into Austrian macroeconomic theory.)[42] To accommodate the analysis of liquidity preferences the structure-of-production diagram must be interpreted so as to include cash balances. In other words, OY must include the quantity of cash balances "consumed." Where a change in time preferences (laborers' and capitalists') will cause both curves of the intertemporal market to shift either east or west, a change in liquidity preferences (laborers' and capitalists') will cause both curves to shift either north or south. A neutral change in liquidity preference would be one in which both curves shifted in such a way as to leave the rate of interest unchanged. The effects of a change in liquidity preferences can be analyzed in terms of the Austrian model of Figure 7, but the details will not be described here. It can be said, however, that the results of such an analysis, whether the change in liquidity preferences is neutral or non-neutral, confront us with no surprises.

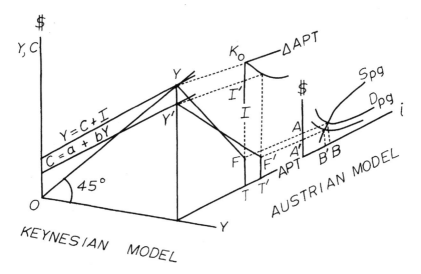

Figure 8

In concluding this section it may be helpful to follow up on the comparison of the Austrian model and the corresponding Keynesian model. The two models are shown in Figure 8 in the same format as was used in Figure 5. There are now two points of commonality. In addition to the common dollar value of consumption goods, the amount of (exogenous) investment in the Keynesian model corresponds in the Austrian model to the amount of (endogenous) investment brought about by a shift in the demand for present goods. Again, the problems created by expressing the Keynesian model in dollar terms rather than real terms are overlooked.

MONETARY DISTURBANCES

To this point it has been implicitly assumed that the economy is free from monetary disturbances. Changes in the endogenous variables were brought about only by actual changes in the preferences of laborers and capitalists, by shifts in the supply and demand for present goods reflecting changes in time (or liquidity) preferences. In this section the supply of money will be introduced as an exogenous variable in the Austrian model, and its effects on the intertemporal market and the structure of production will be analyzed. To facilitate this analysis the actual time and liquidity preferences will be assumed to remain unchanged. The supply and demand for present goods as represented in Figure 3 will be fixed in place throughout the remaining discussion.

In analyzing the effects of monetary disturbances Austrian macroeconomics is not concerned with increases in the quantity of money *per se*, but rather with the process by which the new money enters the economy. According to Hayek: "[E]verything depends on the point where the additional money is injected into circulation."[43] Thus, when Hayek begins his investigation of the " . . . effects of a change in the amount of money in circulation . . .", he immediately turns his attention to the " . . . case most frequently encountered in practice: the case of an increase of money in the form of credits granted to producers."[44] The primary effect of a monetary expansion in the Austrian view stems from the fact that newly created money (credit) tends to fall disproportionately into the hands of producers.

By way of contrast the analysis of a monetary expansion in orthodox macroeconomics is generally begun by assuming that the new money is injected uniformly throughout the economy. A

24

familiar assumption, for instance, is that a helicopter dispenses the newly created money and that individuals dash out into the streets gathering up the new money in direct proportion to the amount they already had.[45] In this sort of highly artificial scenario it can easily be shown that money is neutral. No real magnitudes are changed—apart from a temporary increase in cash holdings that causes *all* prices to be bid up. The only consequence of an increase in the monetary stock, then, is an equiproportional increase in the general price level. Consequences of a nonuniform injection of newly created money, that is, of the fact that some individuals receive a greater share of the new money than others, are categorized as "distribution effects." These effects are considered to be of second-order (or nth order) importance and are generally assumed away in order to get at the "more fundamental" aspects of an increase in the stock of money.[46]

But money in the Austrian view should not be assumed to be neutral and cannot be shown to be neutral in any relevant sense. "The notion of neutral money," according to Mises, is a contradiction in terms: "Money without a driving force of its own would not, as people assume, be a perfect money; it would not be money at all."[47] The relevant question, then, is not whether a monetary expansion is neutral or non-neutral, but rather how the non-neutrality manifests itself in a market economy. The Austrian theorists have focused their attention on this question and have been critical of other monetary theorists for ignoring it. Hayek, for instance, criticized them for focusing " . . . either exclusively or predominantly [on] the superficial phenomenon of changes in the value of money, while failing to pursue the far more profound and fundamental effects of the process by which money is introduced into the economic system, as distinct from its effects on prices in general."[48]

A "neutral" monetary expansion is represented diagrammatically in Figure 9. The vertical axis represents the nominal magnitude of the original stock of money (M_0), i.e., the stock in existence prior to the monetary expansion. The horizontal axis represents the nominal magnitude of the expanded stock of money (M_e), i.e., the stock in existence after the expansion has occurred. The 45° line, representing the equality $M_o = M_e$, serves as a reference. A neutral expansion can be shown, then, by rotating a line clockwise from the reference line.

But if the expansion is achieved by extending newly created credit to producers, it is not a neutral expansion. In the terminology of the present model the newly created money falls disproportionately into the hands of capitalists (as opposed to laborers). This can be represented diagrammatically by showing separately the increase in the quantity of money in the hands of capitalists and the increase in the quantity of money in the hands of laborers. In Figure 10 it is assumed for the sake of simplicity that *all* of the newly created money takes the form of credit extended to capitalists. Initially, then, the laborers are completely unaffected by the monetary expansion. This is represented in Figure 10 by M'_L, which is coincident with the 45° reference line. Capitalists, on the other hand, experience an initially amplified monetary expansion as indicated by M'_c. But

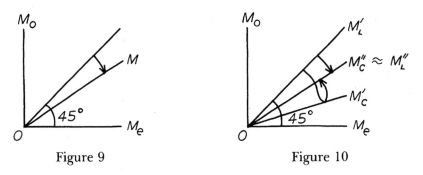

Figure 9   Figure 10

as the capitalists purchase additional quantities of labor services, the new money filters through the economy such that eventually the expansion experienced by the laborers is approximately the same as the expansion experienced by the capitalists. This is indicated by the expansion line $M''_c \approx M''_L$. The arrows indicate the dynamics of the expansion as it appears to the capitalists and to the laborers.

This non-neutral monetary expansion manifests itself as a

26

temporary distortion in the intertemporal market. In terms of the Austrian model the expansion experienced by the capitalists affects the supply-of-present-goods curve, while the expansion experienced by the laborers affects the demand-for-present-goods curve. These two asymmetrical effects can be traced out by the apparatus of Figure 11. The upper panels represent the

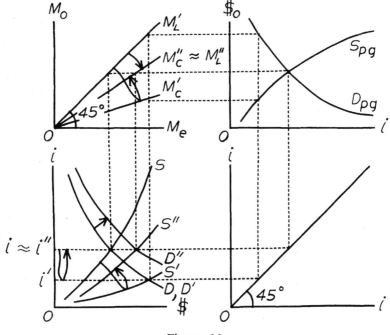

Figure 11

monetary expansion of Figure 10 and the intertemporal market of Figure 3. The southeast panel is a dummy diagram that facilitates the construction of the remaining panel. The southwest panel, then, shows the effect of the monetary expansion on the supply and demand for present goods. The supply curve, reflecting the behavior of capitalists, initially rotates clockwise from S to S^1, while the demand curve, reflecting the behavior of laborers, initially remains in place ($D = D'$). Eventually, though, as the new money becomes more evenly distributed, the supply

27

curve retracts to S'' and the demand curve rotates out to D''. These final positions of the two curves correspond to the expansion line labeled $M''_c \approx M''_L$ in the northwest panel.

Figure 11 illustrates that the rate of interest associated with the "real" parameters remains unchanged, i.e., that the supply and demand curves in the northeast panel remain in place throughout the monetary expansion, while the apparent rate of interest—the rate determined by the southwest panel—does not. The injection of newly created money causes the apparent rate of interest to fall from i to i' and then to rise back to a level approximating the original rate ($i'' \approx i$). This effect of an expansion on the rate of interest is, of course, neither new nor uniquely Austrian. The notion that a monetary expansion causes the interest rate in the loan market to fall temporarily below the "natural" rate is commonly associated with the writings of Wicksell.[49] (It might be added here that the Austrian model does not deny the existence of the Fisher effect. An anticipated increase in the price level would cause a price premium to be built into the nominal interest rate. But the present model abstracts from this price premium just as it abstracts from the price level itself. It focuses instead on relative prices. That the Fisher effect could *completely* offset the other movements in the rate of interest would, of course, have to be denied.)

The intertemporal market, together with the monetary expansion mechanism, can now be reunited with the rest of the Austrian model as shown in Figure 12. All panels are numbered to facilitate the discussion. The only new one is panel VI which simply shows the monetary expansion independent of the process by which the newly created money is injected into the economy. This allows us to express the changes that occur in panels II and III in terms consistent with the original monetary stock, that is, it allows us to focus on relative rather than absolute changes.

The monetary expansion shown in Figure 12 is a neutral one—at least neutral with respect to capitalists and laborers—as indicated by the single expansion line in panel IV. As might be expected this neutral expansion has no effect on the structure of

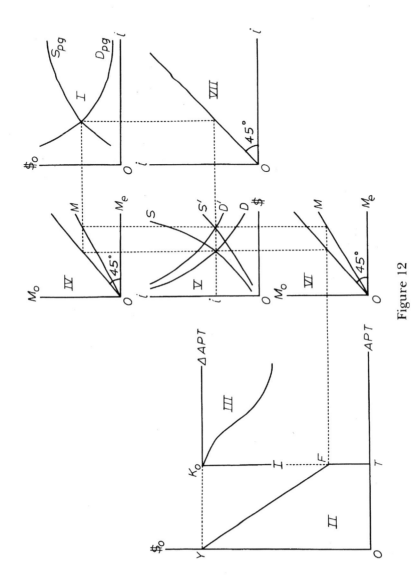

Figure 12

29

production (panel II). Such an "expansion" could be achieved by renaming the monetary unit: From this day on "one Dollar" will be known as "ten Burns." No real changes would result. The only consequence would be the fundamentally uninteresting one (not even shown in Figure 12) that the price level would increase tenfold. The expansion could be achieved instead by using the notorious monetary helicopter. There seems to be no reason to believe that the capitalists would gather up a disproportionate share of the new money. And so, as before, the primary consequence would be an increase in the price level reflecting the extent of the monetary expansion. Two differences, however, make this expansion a little less sterile than the previous one. Firstly, the price level increases not as a matter of definition but as the result of a market process. Prices are bid up to the new level as individuals attempt to draw down their newly acquired cash holdings.[50] Secondly, distribution effects *among* capitalists and *among* laborers are not ruled out. Thus, the consumption goods are valued at OY both before and after the expansion, but they are likely to be different consumption goods and to be consumed by different individuals as a result of these distribution effects. That this is the only change in panel II rests on the heroic assumption that the real-world structure of production is in fact suitable for producing these different consumption goods.

If the increase in the stock of money is achieved by the expansion of credit, there will be a systematic distribution effect that can be accounted for in the Austrian model. The expansion will be experienced first by the capitalists and only later by the laborers. This is illustrated in Figure 13. Unlike the monetary expansion of Figure 12, credit expansion has real effects on the structure of production. Diagrammatically, this is shown by the prime and double-prime notation in panel II. As the apparent rate of interest falls from i to i', the capitalists begin construction of a structure of production that is to have the configuration $OY'F'T'$. But as the newly created money becomes more evenly distributed among capitalists and laborers, the rate of interest rises to i'' ($\approx i$). The beginnings of the longer structure are then

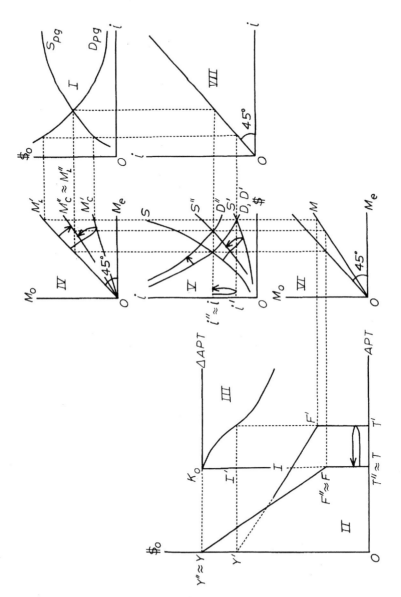

Figure 13

31

liquidated or abandoned in favor of the configuration $OY''F''T''$ which approximates the original structure. The investment (and subsequent dis-investment) represented in panel III by K_0l' is not the result of voluntary saving (and voluntary dissaving) but is the result of the monetary disturbance. This is what Mises termed malinvestment[51] and what Hayek called forced savings.[52]

The changes in the real-world structure of production can be described in terms of the relative profitability of short-term and long-term projects. The economy is assumed to be in equilibrium prior to the monetary expansion so that all projects (short-term and long-term) are equally profitable at the margin. When the interest rate falls, due to the expansion of credit, the long-term projects, which by definition involve disproportionately high interest expenditures, appear to become more profitable. Thus, the capitalists in their entrepreneurial roles bid labor and non-specific capital away from the later stages of production and into the earlier stages and begin construction of whatever specific capital is needed to take advantage of the (apparent) profitability of these long-term projects. But in the very process of constructing the new structure of production the newly created money flows from the capitalists to the laborers, and the distribution of money comes to approximate the old, pre-expansion, distribution. The laborers, whose tastes have remained unchanged, and who now have their full share of the new money, will bid for consumption goods in an amount consistent with the old, pre-expansion, structure of production. That is, they are unwilling to forgo current consumption and to wait instead for the consumption goods associated with the new long-term projects. Their time preferences have not changed. With their bidding for consumption goods the rate of interest rises back to somewhere near its original level. The long-term projects that appeared to be profitable during the expansion are revealed to be unprofitable. The capitalists must act now to cut their losses. The minimizing of losses may require that some of the new long-term projects be completed. Others, however, will have to be liquidated. The specific capital associated with them will have to be abandoned. The laborers and non-specific capital can eventually be reabsorbed in the reconstruction of the original structure of production. But the transition back to the old structure is bound to involve abnormally high levels of unemployed labor and capital.[53]

The two phases of the process that are initiated by a monetary expansion (the first phase corresponding to the prime notation; the second phase to the double-prime notation) should be recognized as the expansion and contraction phases of the business cycle. The above discussion and the diagrammatics of Figure 13 are faithful to Rothbard's capsulization of the cyclical boom and bust:

The "boom" . . . is actually a period of wasteful misinvestment. It is the time when errors are made, due to the bank credit's tampering with the free market. The "crisis" arrives when the consumers come to reestablish their desired proportions. The "depression" is actually the process by which the economy adjusts to the wastes and errors of the boom, and reestablishes efficient service of consumer desires. The adjustment process consists in the . . . liquidation of wasteful investments. Some of these will be abandoned altogether . . .; others will be shifted to other uses . . . .

In sum, the free market tends to satisfy voluntarily-expressed consumer desires with maximum efficiency, and this includes the public's relative desire for present and future consumption. The inflationary boom hobbles this efficiency, and distorts the structure of production, which no longer serves consumers properly. The crisis signals the end of the inflationary distortion, and the depression is the process by which the economy returns to the efficient service of consumers.[54]

And finally, it should be mentioned that to the extent that the malinvestment cannot be recovered there has been a net decrease in the economy's wealth. This can cause real changes in time and liquidity preferences (capitalists' and laborers') resulting in shifts in the supply and demand curves of panel I. To this extent a monetary expansion is not neutral even in the long run.

The Austrian model can be summarized in terms of the diagrammatics of Figure 13. Panels I, II, and III are the basic components of the model. Panel I describes the tastes that are relevant to the macroeconomic variables, i.e., the time and liquidity preferences of capitalists and laborers. Panel II depicts the structure of production that is consistent with the tastes described in panel I. Changes in these tastes will cause the structure of production to undergo a corresponding change subject to the relationship between capital and production time as indicated in panel III. The remaining panels deal with the monetary linkages that translate the individuals' tastes into a corresponding structure of production. In the absence of monetary disturbances the structure of production can be expected to accurately reflect the tastes described in panel I. The presence of a monetary disturbance, however, will prevent these tastes from being accurately reflected in the structure of production. More specifically, an increase in the monetary stock by means of credit expansion will mislead the capitalists into making an (ultimately unsuccessful) attempt to lengthen the structure of production.

FURTHER STUDY

Further development of the Austrian model outlined in this paper could take any of several directions. The effects of various institutional rigidities could be analyzed in terms of the model, for instance, or the model could be modified to take explicit account of expectations of one sort or another. Discussion will be confined here, however, to one particular direction that appears to be potentially fruitful. At the conclusions of earlier sections of this paper the Austrian model was contrasted diagrammatically with the Keynesian model, but no such contrast has been made since the introduction of monetary considerations. The appropriate comparison, then, is one between Figure 13 and some version of the *IS-LM* model. A few comments are in order about how such a comparison might be made.

The key to the comparison of the two models is panel V of Figure 13. The movements of the curves in this panel are suspiciously similar to the movements of the *IS* and *LM* curves. The axes in panel V and in the *IS-LM* diagram measure the same or similar magnitudes, and the conceptualization of the curves in the two models bears a certain resemblance.

In both models the vertical axis measures virtually the same magnitude: *IS-LM* is concerned with the interest rate in the loan market, while panel V measures the apparent rate of interest, which encompasses the loan rate. Where the *IS-LM* diagram measures (real) total income on the horizontal axis, panel V measures (nominal) income of laborers, that is, it excludes interest income. (It is not altogether clear, though, that interest income is actually included in the *IS-LM* diagram in that the Keynesian full-employment income *Y* is the income of *N* workers reckoned in "wage units.")

Further, in elementary formulations of the *IS-LM* model the *IS* curve is frequently conceptualized in a manner consistent with the conceptualization of the corresponding curve in panel V. Dernburg and McDougal, for instance, tell us that " . . . we may . . . interpret the *IS* schedule as the schedule of aggregate demand for goods and services with respect to the interest rate."[55] The rate of interest referred to is clearly the rate in the loan market. It is somewhat less clear, though, whether "goods and services" refers to present (consumption) goods or to all (consumption and investment) goods. If the former interpretation is adopted, the corresponding curves in the two models are very similar indeed. If the latter interpretation is adopted, the actual meaning of the conceptualization is called into question: If the *IS* curve is the demand for all goods, who are the suppliers of all goods, and what are they receiving in exchange for the quantity supplied? (!) The less-elementary macroeconomics texts do not clear up the problem. They usually avoid it by abstaining from any attempt to conceptualize the *IS-LM* curves. They are viewed instead as simply an outgrowth of the graphics that describe the real and monetary sectors of the economy. In a prelude to his discussion of the *IS-LM* diagram Ackley tells us that "[w]e must now throw all these elements into a single pot, stir well, and taste the resulting stew."[56]

Viewing the supply and demand curves of panel V as *LM* and *IS*, respectively, a number of familiar movements of the curves

can be described. A (non-neutral) increase in liquidity preferences, for instance, can shift the LM curve up and to the left,
causing the interest rate to rise; or a (non-neutral) increase in the
willingness to save (decrease in time preference) can shift the IS
curve down and to the left, causing the interest to fall. Changes
in taste will cause real and lasting changes in the IS and LM
curves, but changes in the nominal stock of money will not. A
monetary expansion will shift the LM curve to the right, driving
the rate of interest down, but the monetary stimulation will only
have a temporary effect because the real sector will soon adjust to
the larger monetary stock. The IS curve will also shift rightward,
returning the rate of interest to its original level. A change in the
nominal monetary stock does not cause a real and lasting change
in the rate of interest.

This is not to say that the Austrian model and the IS-LM model
yield the same or similar conclusions or have the same or similar
implications. Quite to the contrary. Equilibrium conditions cannot be defined in terms of panel V of the Austrian model. This
panel shows the movements of the apparent rate of interest and
of the nominal income to laborers during the period that the
economy is experiencing a monetary disturbance. Equilibrium
must be defined in terms of panels I and II, i.e., in terms of the
relevant tastes (time and liquidity preferences) and the structure
of production corresponding to those tastes. It cannot be defined in terms of IS-LM stew. Panel V does open the door,
however, to a thorough comparison of the two models and their
implications.

NOTES

1. Ludwig von Mises, *Human Action: A Treatise on Economics*, 3rd
revised ed. (Chicago: Henry Regnery Co., 1966), pp. 538–86. Also see
Mises, *The Theory of Money and Credit*, trans. by H. E. Batson (New
Haven: Yale University Press, 1953), pp. 339–66. And Mises, "Money,
Inflation and the Trade Cycle: Three Theoretical Studies," trans. by
Bettina Bien Greaves, ed. by Percy T. Greaves Jr. (Unpublished papers, 1923, 1928, and 1931).
2. Friedrich A. von Hayek, *Prices and Production* (New York: Augustus M. Kelley, 1967). Also see Hayek, *Monetary Theory and the Trade*

Cycle, trans. by N. Kaldor and H. M. Croome (New York: Augustus M. Kelley, 1966).

3. Murray N. Rothbard, *Man, Economy, and State: A Treatise on Economics*, 2 vols. (Los Angeles: Nash Publishing Co., 1970), pp. 273–501, 850–81. Also see Rothbard, *America's Great Depression* (Los Angeles: Nash Publishing Co., 1972), pp. 11–38.

4. See, for instance, Don Patinkin, *Money, Interest, and Prices*, 2nd ed. (New York: Harper and Row, Inc., 1965), p. 200.

5. Hayek, *Prices and Production*, p. 34.

6. Gerald P. O'Driscoll, Jr., *Economics as a Coordination Problem: The Contributions of Friedrich A. Hayek* (Kansas City: Sheed Andrews and McMeel, Inc., 1977).

7. Hayek, *Prices and Production*, p. 38.

8. *Ibid.*, p. 36.

9. W. Stanley Jevons, *The Theory of Political Economy*, ed. by R. D. Collison Black (Middlesex: Penguin Books, Inc., 1970), pp. 225–53.

10. Gustav Cassel, *The Nature and Necessity of Interest* (London: MacMillan and Co., Ltd., 1903), pp. 96–157.

11. Eugen von Böhm-Bawerk, *Capital and Interest*, trans. by George D. Huncke and Hans F. Sennholz, 3 vols. (South Holland, Ill.: Libertarian Press, 1959), vol. 2., pp. 10–15 and *passim*.

12. Mises, *Human Action*, pp. 493–503 and *passim*.

13. Hayek, *Prices and Production*, pp. 36–68. Also, see Hayek, *The Price Theory of Capital* (Chicago: University of Chicago Press, 1941), pp. 193–201 and *passim*.

14. Rothbard, *Man, Economy, and State*, pp. 486–92 and *passim*.

15. Jevons, *Theory of Political Economy*, pp. 229–30.

16. *Ibid.*, p. 230.

17. Cassel, *Nature and Necessity of Interest*, p. 54.

18. Rothbard refers to this concept using the term "aggregate production structure." Rothbard, *Man, Economy, and State*, p. 491.

19. Jevons, *Theory of Political Economy*, p. 231.

20. Böhm-Bawerk, *Capital and Interest*, p. 312ff.

21. Mises, *Human Action*, pp. 488–89.

22. Hayek, *Pure Theory of Capital*, p. 140ff. Hayek rejected the notion of aggregate as well as average production time except as the term might be used in a very loose sense. See *Ibid.*, p. 70.

23. Rothbard, *Man, Economy, and State*, p. 412.

24. Hayek, *Prices and Production*, p. 39.

25. *Ibid.*, p. 40.

26. Hayek, *Pure Theory of Capital*, p. 113ff.

27. Mises, *Human Action*, p. 244ff.

28. Rothbard, *Man, Economy, and State*, p. 332.

29. Jevons, *Theory of Political Economy*, p. 227.

30. *Ibid.*, p. 229.

31. See footnotes 20 through 23.

32. Mises, *Human Action*, p. 495.

33. *Ibid.*

34. Rothbard, *Man, Economy, and State*, p. 487.

35. Hayek, *Pure Theory of Capital*, p. 70.

36. G. C. Harcourt and N. F. Laing, eds., *Capital and Growth* (Middlesex: Penguin Books Ltd., 1971), p. 211. Also see G. C. Harcourt, *Some Cambridge Controversies in the Theory of Capital* (Cambridge, England: The Cambridge University Press, 1972), pp. 118–76.

37. John R. Hicks, *Capital and Time* (Oxford: The Clarendon Press, 1973), p. 44.

38. Hayek, *Prices and Production*, pp. 49–54.

39. *Ibid.*, p. 53. Also see Rothbard, *Man, Economy, and State*, pp. 470–79 where similar diagrammatics are used to depict changes in the structure of production brought about by changes in time preferences.

40. Patinkin, *Money, Interest, and Prices*, p. 205.

41. *Ibid.*, pp. 17–21 and *passim*.

42. Friedrich A. von Hayek, *Profits, Interest and Investment* (London: George Routledge and Sons, Ltd., 1939), p. 177.

43. Hayek, *Prices and Production*, p. 11. Hayek reaffirmed this position in his Nobel lecture. See Hayek, *Full Employment at Any Price?* (London: Institute for Economic Affairs, 1975), pp. 23ff. and 37.

44. Hayek, *Prices and Production*, p. 54. See also Mises, *Human Action*, p. 556 and Rothbard, *Man, Economy, and State*, p. 885.

45. Milton Friedman, *The Optimum Quantity of Money and Other Essays* (Chicago: Aldine Publishing Co., 1969), p. 4ff.

46. Patinkin, *Money, Interest, and Prices*, p. 200 and *passim*.

47. Mises, *Human Action*, p. 418.

48. Hayek, *Monetary Theory and the Trade Cycle*, p. 46.

49. It should be pointed out, however, that the Wicksellian "natural" rate is the rate corresponding to a constant price level, while the Austrian "natural" rate is the rate corresponding to the absence of money creation via credit expansion. See Hayek, *Monetary Theory and the Trade Cycle*, pp. 109–16. Also see Rothbard, *Man, Economy, and State*, p. 940.

50. This is the market process that captures Patinkin's attention. Patinkin, *Money, Interest, and Prices*, pp. 236–44.

51. Mises, *Human Action*, pp. 559–61.

52. Hayek, *Prices and Production*, pp. 18–31, and Hayek, *Profits, Interest and Investment*, pp. 183–97.

53. Hayek accounts for this unsuccessful attempt to lengthen the structure of production in terms of the Ricardo effect. See Hayek, *Profits, Interest and Investment*, pp. 8–15. Also see Hayek, "The Ricardo

Effect," *Economica*, IX, No. 34 (new ser.; May 1942): pp. 127–52 reprinted in Hayek, *Individualism and Economic Order* (Chicago: Henry Regnery Co., 1972) pp. 220–54, and Hayek, "Three Elucidations of the Ricardo Effect," *Journal of Political Economy*, 77 (March/April 1969): pp. 274–85.

54. Rothbard, *America's Great Depression*, p. 19. Also see Lionel Robbins, *The Great Depression* (London: The MacMillan Co., Ltd., 1934), pp. 30–54.

55. Thomas F. Dernburg and Duncan M. McDougal, *Macroeconomics* (New York: McGraw-Hill Book Co., 1968), p. 161.

56. Gardner Ackley, *Macroeconomic Theory* (Toronto: The Macmillan Co., 1969), p. 347.

BIBLIOGRAPHY

Ackley, Gardner. *Macroeconomic Theory*. Toronto: The MacMillan Co., 1969.

Böhm-Bawerk, Eugen von. *Capital and Interest*. Translated by George D. Huncke and Hans F. Sennholz. 3 vols. South Holland, Ill.: Libertarian Press, 1959.

Cassel, Gustav. *The Nature and Necessity of Interest*. London: MacMillan and Co., Ltd., 1903.

Dernburg, Thomas F. and McDougal, Duncan M. *Macroeconomics*. New York: McGraw-Hill Book Co., 1968.

Friedman, Milton. *The Optimum Quantity of Money and Other Essays*. Chicago: Aldine Publishing Co., 1969.

Harcourt, G. C. and Laing, N. F., editors. *Capital and Growth*. Middlesex: Penguin Books Ltd., 1971.

Harcourt, G. C. *Some Cambridge Controversies in the Theory of Capital*. Cambridge, England: The Cambridge University Press, 1972.

Hayek, Friedrich A. von. *Full Employment at Any Price?* London: Institute of Economic Affairs, 1975.

Hayek, Friedrich A. von. *Monetary Theory and the Trade Cycle*. Translated by N. Kaldor and H. M. Croome. New York: Augustus M. Kelley, 1966. (First published in 1933.)

Hayek, Friedrich A. von. *Prices and Production*. New York: Augustus M. Kelley, 1967. (First published in 1935.)

Hayek, Friedrich A. von. *Profits, Interest and Investment*. London: George Routledge and Sons, Ltd., 1939.

Hayek, Friedrich A. von. *The Price Theory of Capital*. Chicago: University of Chicago Press, 1941.

Hayek, Friedrich A. von. "The Ricardo Effect," *Economica*, IX, No. 34

(new ser.; May, 1942) 127–52 reprinted in *Individualism and Economic Order*. Chicago: Henry Regnery Co., 1972.

Hayek, Friedrich A. von. "Three Elucidations of the Ricardo Effect," *Journal of Political Economy*, 77 (March/April, 1969): 274–85.

Hicks, John R. *Capital and Time*. The Clarendon Press, 1973.

Jevons, W. Stanley. *The Theory of Political Economy*. Edited by R.D. Collison Black. Middlesex: Penguin Books, Inc., 1970.

Mises, Ludwig von. *Human Action: A Treatise on Economics*, 3rd rev. ed. Chicago: Henry Regnery Co., 1966.

Mises, Ludwig von. "Money, Inflation, and the Trade Cycle: Three Theoretical Studies." Translated by Bettina Bien Greaves, edited by Percy L. Greaves, Jr., unpublished papers, 1923, 1928, and 1931.

Mises, Ludwig von. *The Theory of Money and Credit*. Translated by H. E. Batson. New Haven: Yale University Press, 1953. (First published in 1911.)

O'Driscoll, Gerald P., Jr. *Economics as a Coordination Problem: The Contributions of Friedrich A. Hayek*. Kansas City: Sheed Andrews and McMeel, Inc., 1977.

Patinkin, Don. *Money, Interest, and Prices*. 2nd ed. New York: Harper and Row, Inc., 1965.

Robbins, Lionel. *The Great Depression*. London: The MacMillan Co., Ltd., 1934.

Rothbard, Murray N. *America's Great Depression*. Los Angeles: Nash Publishing Co., 1972. (First published in 1963.)

Rothbard, Murray N. *Man, Economy, and State: A Treatise on Economic Principles*. 2 vols. Los Angeles: Nash Publishing Co., 1970. (First published in 1962.)

About the Author

Roger W. Garrison received the B.S. degree in Electrical Engineering from the University of Missouri at Rolla in 1967. In 1971, after four years of commissioned service in the United States Air Force, he began graduate study in the field of economics and earned the M.A. degree from the University of Missouri at Kansas City in 1973. The Federal Reserve Bank of Kansas City engaged him as a researcher in banking structure until the end of 1974 when he began work on the Ph.D. degree at the University of Virginia. In 1977, the Institute for Humane Studies awarded him a resident fellowship to complete his doctoral dissertation entitled "The Austrian-Neoclassical Relation: A Study in Monetary Dynamics."

Currently, Professor Garrison teaches economics at Auburn University, Auburn, Alabama.